A Girls' Guide to Wisdom and Wealth

What People Are Saying:

Steve Windsor:

I'm in the process of finding mentors and female role models for my daughters to read and emulate. Toni will be on that list. This is a no-nonsense assessment of what anyone, let alone young women should do on their pathway to success. Though Planinsek puts things in terms and with a voice that I have to admit would probably appeal more to my daughters than my own "try hard, set goals, learn who can help you and who's holding you back."

She gets down into some specifics about gender inequality in the workplace and in pay, but never allows that to be used as a crutch for a lack of confidence or progress. Even delving into the law of attraction, she takes a practical approach in breaking it down so the reader can understand it.

It's obvious that her audience is young women looking to start their careers, but the advice strips through that barrier and ends up as solid how-to from a woman who has done a lot in her life and is now on the pathway to giving that success back. Throw in a healthy splash of touchy feely and the book is sure to appeal to young women, starting their financial futures. Great book. Buy it for your daughter be she in high school university or her first job. Neither of you will regret it.

Jonathan C.:
As the parent of a teenage daughter it is important to me that she be taught to manage the money she earns and receives. It's a lesson I didn't learn at her age and while I've made a lot of money over the years, I had, until recently, little to show for it.

Toni Planinsek doesn't just spew information like many top guru's financial books, rather she uses a fictional character named Belinda to illustrate the wisdom and practicality of setting goals for one's future; financially, mentally, spiritually, work, family and more.

More than just a book on money, Toni leverages her years as a teacher and principal at a private girls school, to train young women in how they should think and manage their lives, their money, the work mindsets, and more.

Like a friend coming along-side and distilling sometimes difficult concepts into easy-to-understand language.

I particularly likes chapter 2 where she talked about the influences on young ladies ideas of money and frankly everything comes from family and friends. How a girl and frankly all of us grew up and our parents ideas and practices regarding money have an impact on how we will manager or mis-manage money. We will emulate or learn differently how to handle our earnings, than our parents.

Another chapter that stuck out was "Your Numbers" where she encourages young ladies and again all of us to know our numbers. This might be one of the most important chapters to read and take to heart of most books I've read on financial matters. Toni explores us to know our numbers because they are so critical to our futures and goals. She talks to girls with a positive, encouraging tone that they need to know this info and they're capable enough to learn it.

She finishes the book touching on investing, enough to know about it, but not overly so that one's eyes glaze over. This book is a good, introductory to money mindsets, management and planning for one's future. I highly recommend this to anyone with a daughter or young women who are high school aged or older.

Andy:
A definite book for my daughter, but I would also recommend to men too! Toni has a fantastic writing style,

making this easy to read and interesting.

Sean Sumner:
As the father of 2 girls, I am going to make this part of their required reading before they leave high school. There is great sound advice delivered in a way that anyone can understand.

I love the fact that it is tailored to girls even though it is good advice for anyone, but my girls will see that and feel more of a connection with it and hopefully listen to the advice.

Tish Mellon:
I'm at my first job since graduating from college ... and I don't know anything about money. This is a really helpful book. Toni Planinsek is like a mentor.

G. Mitchell:
If you are a young woman with big dreams - this book is for you, Toni has condensed the wisdom of a great mentor into a book you can access anytime, anyplace. This book will get you armed with all the knowledge you need to plan and navigate your financial future. Everything is explained in simple, easy to understand language - don't let finances and the financial world bamboozle you. If you are not a young woman then buy this book for all the young women in your life and

empower them to make their lives better, and the world a better place in the process.

A GIRLS' GUIDE TO WISDOM AND WEALTH

A Financial Freedom

Quick Start Kit

Thank You

For Your Interest In

A Girls' Guide to Wisdom and Wealth

Please click the link below to receive

Free Bonuses

which support the advice you will find in the book.

http://toniplaninsek.com.au/book-register/

Copyright © 2015 Toni Planinsek

ISBN -13: 978-1512245424

ISBN-10: 1512245429

All rights reserved. No part of this publication may be reproduced, distributed, or transmitted in any form or by any means, including photocopying, recording, or other electronic or mechanical methods, without the prior written permission of the publisher, except in the case of brief quotations embodied in reviews and certain other non-commercial uses permitted by copyright law.

www.toniplaninsek.com.au

For orders please email orders@toniplaninsek.com.au

DEDICATION

For all the women and girls in my small tribe:

Kate, Elizabeth, Rebecca,

Maddie, Sarah B, Hannah, Charlotte,

Sarah, Sophie and Isabelle

Disclaimer

This publication contains the opinions and the ideas of the author. It is sold with the understanding that neither the author nor the publisher is engaged in rendering legal, tax, investment, insurance, financial, accounting or other professional advice or services. If a reader requires such advice or services, a competent professional should be consulted. Relevant laws vary from state to state. The strategies outlined in this book may not be suitable for every individual and are not guaranteed or warranted to produce any particular results. Both the author and publisher specifically disclaim any responsibility for any liability, loss or risk, personal or otherwise, which is incurred as a consequence, directly or indirectly, of the use and application of any of the contents of this book.

Introduction

You are a motivated, modern young woman. You have already started to have some successes. You are determined to continue with your success and to be rich and independent.

The problem is that you don't know what to do next.

I have your answer. In *A Girls' Guide to Wisdom and Wealth*, I show you how you can continue your success well into the future. I give you strategies for taking complete control of your life and achieving your dream lifestyle.

It can be a big dream. In this exciting new digital world we are now totally aware of what people are achieving all over the world. This new view of everything has allowed us to imagine futures, which were never possible before. There is a lot of opportunity now to have and do things that your parents didn't know existed. In the past these opportunities may not have been feasible for a young person, particularly a female.

I have been educating and working with women and girls most of my professional life. Time and time again I have observed that what most young women want, is financial freedom. They want to be rich not only for the money but for what it represents. They want the freedom to travel, to be able to have the material things they like, financial security and the lifestyle that they want to choose for themselves.

In *A Girls' Guide to Wisdom and Wealth* I will explain in an easy to read and understand manner how you can create your own wealth and live your own dream. In the past girls weren't always encouraged to think outside what were considered traditional female roles. Those days are gone. Today you can do whatever you choose.

What is particularly exciting is that you can start now, no matter what your current circumstances are.

The number of female entrepreneurs is growing daily. You may be an entrepreneur already or perhaps you are thinking of becoming one. Unfortunately there have not been as many financially independent women as men to learn from. Even at school or from your family there may not have been a lot of finance information available for you.

I am providing a great resource with some tricks, tips and

methods for today's young female high achievers. It is a starter kit with some sound and dependable advice to you started on the right path to realising your dreams.

In *A Girls' Guide to Wisdom and Wealth* you will find the secrets to how you can plan and achieve all these things for yourself. Your success won't depend on anyone else. You will have complete control of your own finances.

I promise you that when you read this book, you will be motivated and confident. You will be savvy with money. You will be able to live a balanced, organised and fulfilling life. You will know and understand how the Law of Attraction works and how it can contribute to your success.

Part of the success formula for young women to be independent and wealthy is to make a decision and act. Thinking about it will not bring the changes you want. So take action now and start reading.

Before you know it, you will see positive changes in your life. You will be comfortable with your financial situation, and you will see your income grow quickly. The sooner you start this journey, the sooner you reach that destination—the one where you are rich enough to have financial freedom. You will then be able to live the lifestyle you desire.

Table of Contents

Chapter 1: Creating Your Dream Future

Your Goals

You want to be successful. You want to be have the freedom to follow your dreams yet still be financially secure. There is a way. You will be able to do it with this book as your guide.

Success leaves clues. For you to be successful, the trick is to find the clues then follow them. You can find the clues by reading about successful people, watching them and asking them directly. What are common threads? Are there habits, behaviours or activities that are common to them all?

One thing that all top achievers have are goals. They know what they are trying to achieve. They know the destination they are aiming for. They write their goals down and refer to them often.

> *Belinda is 24. She had been doing some personal training work and had just started doing Boot Camps with young women in school halls and in parks. She was enjoying it but she thought she could do more.*

Research studies show a direct link between goals and enhanced performance in business. The same applies generally in other areas of living, not just business.

Harvard University has done several long-term studies looking at the success of graduates who wrote down their goals at the end of their courses and those graduates who did not.

> *Belinda decided she would like to have her own studio with other instructors working there as well. She decided that this was how she wanted to spend her time and she wanted to make a successful business of it.*

The average success in business and earnings of the group with written goals was much higher than the average success of those without written goals. The very act of writing down goals improved graduates' chances of reaching higher levels in organisations or in their own businesses and earning more money.

The Pen is Mightier ...

Imagine that—all you need to do is write down your goals, and you have taken your first big step towards your success. It sets the process in motion.

> *Belinda put aside a day to really think through how she wanted her business to be in eight to ten years. She decided that by then she would be able to have at least two studios with classes from six in the morning until nine at night. She calculated how many instructors and clients would be needed to make this a success.*

When you write clear, well-defined goals, you are making it possible to measure your progress towards achieving the goals. It is like having your own roadmap. Without goals you have a sense of being adrift. It leads to a sense of frustration because you feel like you are not getting anywhere. You have no markers of achievement along the way.

Goals:

- Help you focus and by having them you are more likely to allocate your time and resources more efficiently.

- Help you stay motivated when things get a little tough, as is likely from time to time. You are less likely to just give up when you know you have a destination you are heading towards.

Your Course

An aeroplane travelling between two cities is on course a very small percentage of the time. The majority of its time is involved in getting back on course as a result of what the wind and air pressure do to the aeroplane.

You and your goals are like those aeroplanes. If you know where you are going, you can focus on the end result and get back on track when obstacles appear. Without a clear destination you would be knocked off course. Eventually you will land somewhere but probably nowhere near where you wanted to go.

Goals remind you what you are expecting of yourself, and they leave you nowhere to hide when your performance drops. However, by setting and achieving goals, you will experience the feeling of success, and this in turn spurs you on to improved productivity and confidence.

> *Now that Belinda had decided what her long-term target was she thought about what the halfway mark would be like. By then she would have one studio operating. This goal was closely aligned with her financial goals. What would the expenses and income of the business be? What*

was the profit she wanted? Did that make sense with the numbers she would have?

Achieving Your Goals

Without specific written goals you have no way of actually knowing how well you are doing. This is why so many people just cruise along. They have dreams of a better life, and they do have some kind of idea where they want to go, but it is not specific.

The difference between living and achieving your dreams and just living an average life is the quality of the goals you set for yourself—and these goals have to be recorded in writing.

Studies have shown that around 95% of adults will have never written a goal in their lives. Can you imagine? Setting and writing goals are so important, yet almost no one does it.

Goals are not just important, they are super important. By just writing out your goals, you put yourself amongst that small percentage of adults who go on to achieve their dreams.

Putting Your Dreams Into Words

So what are these goals, which we know are so important? Goals are how you achieve the life you want to live in the future. Because each of us is different, each of us has a different vision of the life we want to have.

The goals you choose need to be yours and yours alone. Often we go along with our parents' or friends' ideas of what we should be aiming for. These would not be authentic goals. You need to be connected at a deeper level with the goals you choose. They should be what you dream of in your heart of hearts. You probably have been thinking of them for some time.

Your goals should be feasible and aligned, meaning that they can't contradict each other. It would be counterproductive to have a goal of doing record times as a marathon runner and having another goal of living a life with little exercise. One goal would work against the other.

Each of your goals contributes one aspect or piece of the larger picture of your future life. It is important that the goals set by you are consistent with your values. You are setting yourself up for failure if the goals you set go against what you believe in.

Goals need to be expressed in positive language. It's important to always be positive because you are sending a message to your subconscious. Your subconscious doesn't understand the difference between positive and negative. It just follows instructions, so if you're setting a destination plan, the more positive the instructions, the more positive the results.

Goals should only be about you. Do not have a goal that is against someone else. Goals should not be a vendetta. Writing goals should be a positive, uplifting experience. You should 'feel' right about them.

All the Details

Be specific. All the details about each goal need to be filled in. If you dream of owning a home, just to say, 'I want a home,' is not good enough. You need to describe the home. Explain how many bedrooms there are, what it looks like on the outside and what it has on the inside. The more detail you can give for each item, the better your subconscious understands what it is that you are aiming for.

This is not a two-minute exercise, and it may take a while to think through exactly every aspect of each goal and then write it out in detail. That's probably why most people don't ever write them down because it does take some effort.

> *In doing this exercise Belinda also realised that the income she could earn would be limited to the number of clients and classes she could fit into one or more buildings. It was then she started to understand the impact of having other forms of income as well.*

I have found that by writing goals out, my mind starts to go over and over them, and I find myself going back and tweaking them a bit. Enjoy the process and let it spread over a few days, so you can start to zero in on the specifics.

Measuring

Each goal needs to be measurable. Along the way you will want to be able to see the progress you have made. Having a goal of being happy is fine, but how do you measure how close you are to achieving it? So turn it around in your head and explore it a little. Then list the things that would make you happy. If you can qualify the goal in terms of dollars or time or in some tangible way, that makes it easier to see how you are tracking towards reaching the goal.

You have to be the one who achieves the goal with your own efforts. You have no control over the actions of others, so it should not depend on anyone else's efforts except your own.

> *The first year goals, which Belinda wrote, were very specific. She had to research the best location for a studio, decide on the best space which was on offer, do a business plan so she could calculate how many clients she would need to cover expenses and make some money.*

The Complete You

It is difficult to achieve and enjoy success in one aspect of our life if another aspect is going badly. Having lots of money isn't worth much if you are too ill to enjoy it.

Imagine the whole you as a large wheel. There are seven spokes coming from the centre to the outer rim of your wheel. Give each spoke a name:

1. Mind/Mental
2. Body/Physical
3. Spirit/Your Inner Self
4. Work/Career
5. Money/Finances
6. Social
7. Family/Relationships

Think about each of these aspects of your life. How well is it going at the moment? Are you happy with that aspect of your life? Is it the way you want it to continue into the future?

Give it a score out of ten, with ten being the highest. On a piece of paper draw a small circle as the centre of your wheel. Then draw each spoke out from the centre in proportion to its score. If you gave yourself a two for family, then that will be a very short line. Do this for each heading. Then join the outer ends of the spokes.

This gives you a visual representation of how well-rounded your life is at the moment and which areas may need the most work.

If you gave yourself a two for each, you would have a perfect circle but what a small little wheel. We want you to have the biggest life possible. So think BIG. Don't put limits on yourself. We often do that because those around us have convinced us not to dream.

Opportunity to Reflect

The next step is to think how you would like that area of you life to be. I found I gave myself a very low score on how well my family life was going when I did this exercise for the first time. I always meant to do things with my children, but often it didn't happen because I was too busy with work and other things kept getting in the way. Yet if I had been asked, I would have said my children were the most important thing in my life.

When I actually wrote goals under my "family" heading, which were specific and measurable, things began to change. I didn't just write that I wanted a better relationship with my family. I wrote details of what I wanted our relationship to look like and what activities we should be doing. Then I could measure how things were going. I often had to adjust what I was doing when I found myself going off course. Having the lists to reread continually reminds you of what is important.

This is your opportunity to think deeply about each part of your life. As we move through the book, possible ideas for goals under each of these headings will become clearer.

Belinda is a smart cookie. She knows that her

work and finance goals are going to dominate her life a bit in the next few years as she builds her business, but she also knows she wants to keep in contact with her large Italian family. She believes she can manage a balanced life, which includes fun and laughter, by making sure she plans for time with loved-ones and friends. She has planned for travel and holidays.

Length of Time

I suggest doing three sets of goals. Each set will be for a different time period. I start with the long-term ones, which for me is eight to ten years. I list my detailed goals under each of the headings. Then I consider what these will look like in three to five years if I am on track, and I write these out as medium-term goals. Then lastly I set goals for one year out.

This exercise is for you and you alone. No one but you will be checking. The very worst thing you can do is to lie to yourself. Make your goals a bit of a stretch but not completely unattainable. You don't need to know how it is all going to happen at this point. The universe has a role to play in this process, and we will discuss that role later. It might amaze you.

Belinda was so excited because she could see the path forward now for the work section of her life. She aligned her financial goals and her mental goals as well. She became determined to know her numbers. She actually broke the first year into three-month blocks and then did her weekly planning to ensure she met those quarterly goals.

Indulge Yourself

I like making this process very special, so I bought a small, very beautiful journal to write my goals in. It is astounding when you look back on what you wrote to see how it all unfolded. Many of my goals were reached in ways I could not have imagined. The universe delivered things I had not even thought of and they were better than I had listed. Being flexible and trusting the process are both crucial.

Update Your Goals

Once you have completed these goals and you are happy with them, they do not get put in the bottom drawer and forgotten. They should be kept in a place where you can read through them regularly. You may find you will want to make slight adjustments as time passes.

When I wrote mine in my journal, I spread the headings evenly through the whole book. Then I put the date I was writing them and made the list, with all the details for each heading. Later on because some unexpected things happened and I wanted to change a couple, I just put the new date under the existing list and noted the changes.

Remember—in 12 months you will be redoing the short-term ones.

Vision

Having a vision of what you want and referring to it regularly are parts of the process. I am not a very visual person, so I took up the idea of having a pinboard with illustrations of what I wanted. Every time I saw something in a magazine that fit my dream, up it went on the pinboard.

Some people are listmakers, and some people are not. If you are not, you need to start doing it. I advocate doing some planning each week. Stephen Covey's idea of weekly planning, which he shares in *The Seven Habits of Highly Effective People*, is the basis of the planning method I use.

To tell it simply, he gives the example of a teacher showing her students a large empty glass jar. The teacher then fills it with big rocks right up to the brim and asks the class if it is full. They all say it is. Then the teacher brings out a container with very small pebbles and shakes the jar as she pours and lots go in. 'Now is it full?' she asks. This time the class is satisfied that it is indeed full. But out comes some sand, which the teacher manages to add to the jar. She smooths it across at the top of the jar.

The class applauds, and now the students are absolutely sure the jar is as full as it could possibly be. Wait, the teacher now brings out a pitcher of water and proceeds to pour it into the jar.

Each week is like that jar. You can fit an enormous amount in if you plan it correctly and know your priorities.

The big rocks are the most important things you have to do in the coming week. They go in first. The pebbles are the next most important things, and so on down the list. Imagine if you filled your week with sand and water-type things and then tried to get any big rocks in—it would be impossible to achieve. To me sand and water activities are all those time-waster things, which we often let eat up our time when we know we should be doing other things. You know that feeling—busy being busy but not really doing anything.

Your Big Rocks

Stephen Covey has a suggestion for ensuring you cover all your headings when you are thinking of what your 'big rocks' might be for this week. He says we each have different hats that we wear for each major role we have in life. You may have the hat of a daughter, you may also be a wife, a grandchild, a worker and so on. For my work, I subdivided it into the different functions I performed at work.

List the major roles you have. My 'mother' hat was one of mine, so when one of my children was in a musical concert at school, that was a 'big rock' to me and I made sure it went in the diary first. You may have an important work meeting that simply can't be missed. It's a 'big rock', so put it in early.
These 'big rocks' don't just have to be about work. They are about moving you towards any of your goals. One of your 'big rocks' for the week might be catching up with an old friend. This system is meant to ensure you integrate all aspects of your life into your diary.

The process doesn't have to be arduous. I keep a list of all my 'hats' on the inside cover of my diary, and as I sit with my diary on Sunday night, I mentally run down the list to remind myself what I need to be putting in the diary for the coming week.

When you allocate yourself some time to just sit and think, you allow yourself the opportunity to hear that little voice in your head make suggestions. An idea may just pop into your mind. I will say more about learning to listen to and use the advice of that little voice in following chapters.

Chapter 2: Your Circle of Influence

Family Influence

We need to talk about your family because growing up, they were your greatest influence. You may not realise that most of your beliefs and habits have come from what you learned from them when you were a child. We tend to think that everybody has the same experiences as us and that they will think and behave the same as us. It comes as a shock as we go through school to discover that not all families have the same beliefs and habits.

Think about marriage. What did you learn about marriage from your parents? Did they have a happy marriage when you were little? If it was, you probably have positive feelings towards marriage. If there were fights and tension, you may have a different view of marriage completely.

The same goes for your siblings. In some families there is a close bond between brothers and sisters whereas in other families there may be constant fights, jealousy and very little affection and cooperation.

Think back on things that happened in your family as you

were growing up. What messages did you get about your education and your work or career? Were there strong opinions about which jobs were valid and appropriate, particularly for you as a girl?

University studies suggest that the relationship between the family's influence and ethnic identity is more pronounced for females than males. This is consistent with previous research suggesting that parents tend to focus on passing on cultural traditions to daughters more than to sons. This is not good news if the ethnic group has strong negative attitudes about women and their financial independence.

Family Money

How did your family connect work and money? Did both parents work outside the home? Did they have stable jobs? In some families there is conflict about work. Some people have the attitude that the world owes them a living, and they are very happy to live on benefits rather than go to work. In other families they may love the work they do, so their attitude is completely different. Work is a joy to them.

Did you hear criticism of people who worked hard and were ambitious? Were people who had more money resented?

I want you to reflect on how money was viewed in your family. Was it discussed openly? Was it shared fairly? Who controlled the money in your family? Was it valued and saved or was it gambled and wasted? Who was accountable for the money in your family?

Was there any guilt surrounding work and money? Do you feel you owe something to your family because of things you received when you were a child? Was a debt discussed?

All of these behaviours gave you a model of the world. Now you need to identify which of these messages you have kept and are influencing your attitude to work and money today. If they were the wrong kind of messages, they will stop your moving forward.

This is your opportunity to wipe the slate clean, look around you and realise that there are other more positive ways to view work and money.

Your Way

When you wrote your goals, I reminded you that these goals were to be yours. You must not set goals to win the approval of your family or friends. You are your own person, and you must put yourself first.

If you have ever flown in an aircraft, you will have heard the attendant say you must put on your own oxygen mask before you try to help anyone else. That can be difficult as we are constantly getting the message that we should put others first.

You may love your parents very much and want to do things for them. That is fine, but it needs to be after you have made yourself secure. The best way to do that is to be authentic about what you choose to do. Your job is to be happy. You will achieve that if your follow your own passion.

You may be fortunate enough to have parents who will support you in reaching your goal. Unfortunately, many families are dysfunctional, and you may find that they are jealous of your success and try to bring you down. In these circumstances you need to be careful how much time you spend with them.

Some people manage to be able to be with their family and not let their opinions or advice deter them from their goal. Others find that over time they drift away from their family as they have very little in common and they tire of the negativity.

Often your success can make them feel uncomfortable, as it highlights what they haven't achieved. That is their problem, not yours. If it feels unsafe to share what you are working on, don't share. Don't waste your energy trying to convert them to your way of thinking. Keep your own counsel and stay focused. If there is no support from within the family, you will need to seek it elsewhere.

Friends

Your friends are like your family in many ways. They have an influence on your habits and behaviour. The good thing about friends is that you get to choose them whereas you have no choice with your family.

Good friends will encourage you in your endeavours to reach your goals. Sometimes friends pretend to support you but will continually try to tempt you into behaviours that work against your reaching your goals. You see this often when someone decides to lose weight, and instead of helping, the friends keep tempting the person with fatty treats.

Look at the behaviour of your friends carefully. If they are indeed true friends, you will be able to share with them your successes and failures. You won't feel you have to hide things from them.

You have a vision of what you want your future life to look like. Does the current behaviour of your friendship group fit that vision? There is a saying if you want to be rich, do what rich people do. If your current friends don't have similar goals, you will find it more difficult to pursue your goals.

The ways you speak, dress and generally behave now affect your future. Choose your friends carefully. It may be necessary to leave some behind. If you do have to find a new friendship group, think about where you would meet people with similar goals to your own.

If you are starting a business of your own, look for groups for young businesswomen. In groups like this you will find women with similar objectives who will encourage you and help build your confidence. Often women's fitness groups help in the same way. Athletes or fitness participants can be good at setting goals and working towards them. It is great to have a buddy who encourages you when you have one of those down moments.

Focus on the positive attributes you would like in a friend. If you display the same attributes to others, you will attract the kind of friends you are looking for—friends that build you up, applaud your success and generally make you feel good about yourself.

If no one in your current extended friendship group is living the life you want, you likely won't live that desired lifestyle. On the other hand, if everyone in your group is living by your values, then you will more quickly reach your goals. This is the sphere of influences in our lives.

For example, if you spend more time watching *The Kardashians*, eventually your brain will infer that these individuals are members of your group or tribe. The values they live by become your values. This is all fairly unconscious; you wouldn't think an image on a television screen affects you in this way, but your brain doesn't know the difference.

Be mindful of who you spend your time around and what you watch on television, Youtube or social media. These influences have more effect then you think. The good thing, at least in the case of Youtube and social media, is that you can filter these platforms to the point where you are surrounded by those with similar values to yours.

Chapter 3: Work Is Not The Only Way

Our civilisation has been built on work. Through the work mankind has done, we can track our collective evolution from the first tools man made to where we are today. How we understand the meaning of the word has also changed through the ages.

We have the need within us to strive, create and build. We need to work. What makes us happy is doing things with some purpose. We like to have the feeling that what we are doing is meaningful.

Workplace Equality

Traditionally the work of men and women was divided. The work done by women was not rewarded financially the same as men even if they did exactly the same work. I could write a whole book on this very subject. For the moment, let's recognise that things are slowly improving for women. Things are still not equal in many fields, so we must continue to press for equality. Women should have as many viable work options as men. Equal work should mean equal pay.

Be Confident

Studies show that women are sometimes their own worst enemies when it comes to assessing their own abilities, especially in the workplace. Even from a young age females underestimate their abilities while males overestimate their abilities. Women don't apply for jobs unless they have 100% of the required skills whereas males will apply with only 60% of the skills asked for. Women have lacked the same level of confidence that men have.

Women aim to achieve perfectionism, and when they perceive themselves as not being perfect, they don't act or take a risk thinking they are not yet ready. This comes from old thinking that has women continually looking for external approval in the workplace. Generally women don't have the confidence habit in the workplace.

The confidence habit can be learned. Without it women will not achieve their true potential. All successful women show that they have the confidence habit.

The more you practise, the better you get. Each action you take to strengthen this habit gives you the confidence to take the next action step, and so your confidence grows.

Comfort Zone

Firstly you need to connect you and your work with a greater purpose. What's your purpose? What will it achieve for you and others?

The second step to develop the confidence habit is to tap into your passion and be prepared to take risks. Push yourself outside of your comfort zone. Don't worry if not all things you try work. I have heard successful women say, 'Fail fast and fail often', and you will learn lots. You have to accept that failing is part of the learning process.

Then surround yourself with great people. Don't think you have to do everything alone. Even if you start your own business and it is just you—look for ways to get the advice of others. Choose a mentor and actively seek out people you can learn from and who can help you achieve your goals.

Be Progressive

Innovation and change happens in work practices just like it happens everywhere else. The way you do your work will need to change to keep up. The best way to have confidence that you are current is to be a perpetual learner. Look for courses and other ways to keep yourself up-to-date. Knowing what is happening is a sure way to build your confidence.

Lastly take action. Just doing it bolsters our belief in our ability to succeed. Then success itself bolsters our confidence, and so the cycle continues.

The biggest obstacle to having confidence is our own self-doubt. We are often quick to feel we are a fraud or it is a fluke we have succeeded. Don't believe it. You can learn this confidence habit, and you won't feel like an impostor. You will achieve your success in your work because you deserve it.

Love Your Work

People who are very happy doing what they do will often say it's not like going to work at all, they enjoy it so much. There is that underlying suggestion that if it is fun and you are enjoying it, then it can't be work. Along with this is the attitude that it is almost wrong to take money for doing things you enjoy.

This is the thinking I want you to recognise in yourself and others. Make the decision right now to change this belief.

You need to work to gain fulfilment in your life. There needs to be a sense of purpose to your work. You need money to finance the lifestyle you desire. There is nothing wrong in combining all these aspects.

The current wisdom is that if you do something you love, then the money will follow. This is a charming sentiment, but a smart woman realises that there does need to be some viability in the marketplace—that is assuming that money is the only goal. I suggest it is not the money but what it represents.

Patience

Thankfully the workplace has changed in Western society, but positive change has not been uniform, and many people still seem to feel trapped and unhappy in their workplace. They dream of not having to work. If they had the money to be completely idle, would that make them happy?

In our society our job helps us define our identity. So having no work at all does not necessarily equate to happiness. I think it is better to broaden our definition of work and find an activity we can happily do and call it work.

In recent years we have demanded more and more instant gratification. This has happened with our work as well. Work sometimes needs to be considered in the context of a lifetime or at least a reasonable amount of time. For some work, it may be just impossible to achieve success by next week. Many types of work need the type of skills, which are practised and improved over time, so that the building of this expertise gives the worker joy and a sense of achievement.

Bespoke items are back in fashion. There is real

constructiveness in this type of work. The workers making these pieces of clothing, furniture and other items have built up their skills over time. They take pride in their work.

The same might happen in a business you start for yourself. Take a longer view of what success might look like. Give yourself the time to build your skills and expertise. Great businesses don't happen over night.

New Jobs

In my parents' generation the work someone did when they left home was strongly influenced by the work that other members of the family did. Miners' sons went into the mines, the butchers' sons worked in their fathers' shops and so on. Educational opportunities were very limited and so too were the choices.

For my generation things changed radically, particularly for girls. A minority of us was able to go to university, and this meant a much wider choice of work. There was still a strong push for girls to choose the serving professions like teaching and nursing. Girls were still seen to be inferior in those 'brainy' subjects like mathematics and science.

There were so many jobs for my generation that we could pick and choose. That started to change as a larger percentage of young people was able to gain postsecondary training. There was competition for work, and some jobs were seen to be superior as you could earn more money in those.

If you received a high score at the end of high school, you were encouraged to enter these elite and highly prized courses as it was considered a waste of your final scores otherwise.

At one of the girls' private schools where I was teaching, there were at least four of the teachers in senior school, who had been dux (the top student academically) of their high schools and then they went into teaching. That is most unlikely to happen these days. If a girl were dux of her school and she chose to enter a kindergarten teachers' course, people would say she was 'wasting' her high score, meaning they think she should have gone for the course which gives the qualifications for the highest paying job.

Sometimes we are in a position where we do have to work just for the money. If that is short-term to achieve a goal, it may be perfectly fine. Don't ever choose your life's work for this reason. It is soul-destroying to spend the majority of your life doing work you dislike or even hate, even if it pays good money.

It is important that you know what you want to achieve, so you can plan the best type of work for you.

Financial Freedom to Choose

What are success and wealth going to mean to you? I am not assuming that you are necessarily equating money with wealth. You need to paint a picture of yourself in your mind of how you want your life to look.

It is fine to choose to do work that makes you happy. Will that work provide the financial rewards that will provide the other things you want in your life? Many artistic people choose to spend a lot of their time doing their art form, which may provide little financial means initially. It may be a constructive type of work, which means they will need to improve their skills and competence before they reach the expertise level, which results in more financial rewards. In the short-term they may need to do supplementary work to finance their current lifestyle.

I think the majority of workers in restaurants and bars are doing this kind of work.

The ultimate goal is to be doing work that is your passion, so it doesn't feel like 'traditional work' at all and to receive enough money to do what you want with your life.
The core thing is to think through what you do want to spend your time doing. Then work out how to finance that.

Don't be concerned if it isn't well paying in the beginning. We will discuss doing the best with any money you do earn more in later chapters.

No Jobs For Life

In previous times the job or profession you started with was the one you finished with. In fact it was seen as a very positive thing to stay in a job for 30 plus years. There may have been changes of roles within the organisation, but staying with the one company was applauded. That has changed. Not only do people change the work they do, they change with whom they do it.

Don't be afraid to change your mind. Each experience adds to your knowledge base and is useful. I always say that knowledge is no burden to carry nor is experience. Taking a risk and trying something out is worthwhile. Much better than spending a lifetime wondering if you could have done something for yourself.

When I had breast cancer for the first time, I gave up being a school principal. I was terrified as I couldn't imagine what other work I could possibly do. I had been in schools since I'd left school. Then I discovered business, and a whole new world opened up.

Expect Change

With the rate of change speeding up many of the jobs that were around when I was young no longer exist. Now there are jobs we couldn't have even imagined back then.

You have to be flexible and accept that change may be forced upon you. That is the kind of change, which is more difficult to adjust to. If you initiate the change, it has to be exciting and fulfilling. Look to be in control as much as you can and watch for trends.

That is another good reason to be continually learning. Don't assume because a business works today, that it is going to look the same in ten or twenty years. Whether you decide to work for yourself or for someone else, I want you to think of yourself as your own company. When you do work for yourself, you become very aware of what you have to do to be successful. It is obvious that you have to continually learn new things to run your own business.

When you work for someone else, have the same attitude. Invest in yourself. Do your best and keep learning. Understand the laws that affect 'You Inc.'. Understand the taxes and pay scales associated with it. If you were actually starting your own business, you would need to learn a lot more than just about the product or service you were going to sell. Initially you will need all the skills for running a small business.

Don't allow your performance to be negatively influenced by others. One of the real estate gurus in Australia, John McGrath, tells the story of how when he started leasing properties, the average number of leases his colleagues did was fairly low. He decided to go for it and did more than double the number they did. He wasn't popular with the others, but he saw himself as his own company, and he wasn't going to underperform just to make it easy for his colleagues. Be true to yourself and always put in your best effort.

Chapter 4: Attracting What You Want

Law of Attraction

You have probably heard of the Law of Attraction and the Power of Intention. You may have thought these were a fairly new topic of general chitchat, featured in magazine articles and books. It may not have always been referred by these names, but there is evidence that mankind has always understood the meaning behind this Law and how it works. Attracting what you believe in is written about in most religious and wisdom literature including the Christian Bible.

What do they mean? Briefly they mean we attract what we think about. The part of the Law that comes, as a bit of a surprise, is that this Law teaches that every positive or negative event that has happened to you was attracted by you. If some terrible things have been happening to you, it may be hard to accept that you actually brought them into your own life.

The Law is working all the time, so even if we are thinking of it or not, it continues to work. Your thoughts are very powerful. You can only think one thought at a time. You need to make sure that you are thinking only positive thoughts.

The challenge is to be sure about what you want, decide what you want to do and then don't doubt yourself. Each time you think about reaching your goals, you are sending a request to the universe.

The Universe

Albert Einstein told us that 'everything is energy'; that 'a human being is a part of the whole called by us the Universe'. His words echoed the most ancient of spiritual and philosophical teachings, which still underpin today's cutting-edge scientific discoveries. The Universal Mind goes by many names. In the scientific world it is the Unified Field, in spiritual philosophy we refer to The All, Source or Universal Consciousness and in religion we call upon God who Himself goes by many names—Jehovah, Allah and Brahman, to mention but a few. The name is relevant only in so far as it resonates with you.

You have a two-way connection to the universe through your thoughts. You need to learn how to send clear messages to the universe. You need to learn how to recognise the universe working in your life.

The level of importance you put on the reasons for wanting something is going to activate the Power of Intention. Intention is very powerful because it acts like a magnet. The more passionate you are, the higher your energy or vibrations will be.

If you do not have strong enthusiasm and you are not

clear or a little unsure of what you want, then the universe will receive an unclear frequency. You will see unwanted results.

Gratitude

Being thankful for what you already have in your life is an important element of training your thoughts for the good. We often completely take for granted all the things we have already received. Keeping a journal in which you write three or more things every day that you are grateful for is a good way to remind yourself of the positive things in your life.

If you have trouble thinking of things, try mentally taking away some things that you already have, such as your sight, hearing, first cup of coffee in the morning or yesterday's sunset. When you think about it in this way, the list of things to be grateful for is almost endless. Then imagine each of these items coming back into your life one by one. I know you will be grateful.

Gratitude particularly holds true when it comes to finances. To have abundance, be grateful for and properly manage whatever wealth you have now, even if you don't think it's much. If you're not appreciating what you already have, you aren't probably using it wisely. If you can't do that, why should the universe believe you can handle more money?

New Habits

Controlling your thoughts, being continually grateful and understanding the power of intention may all be new ideas in your life. You will need to practise these on a regular basis, so they become habits, which you don't have to think about. You will just do them automatically, and you will start to see the amazing power of the Law of Attraction manifest in all aspects of your life.

The Process

There are three basic steps to the Law of Attraction:

1. Ask
2. Allow
3. Receive

That sounds simple, doesn't it? It is, if you understand each step and you do it correctly.

1. Ask

This is the easy part I think. You've written your goals. You should by now know exactly what you want. You need to be clear in your message to the universe. That is why it was so important to write out your goals in detail.

Some people find visualisation can help in this step. You can make a noticeboard on which you put illustrations or photos of the things you are aiming for. The clearer the picture you have in your head of the life you want to live, the better the chance you have of achieving it.

You are producing your own movie of your life in the future, yet as you watch this movie, you need to see it as if it has already happened. You use present tense as if you already have it.

If one of your goals is to be rich, is it the money you want or what you think it represents? Are you talking about money or freedom? Having money does not necessarily mean having more freedom, security or peace of mind. There are plenty of rich people who are completely miserable. They may have little freedom.

I suggest what you really want is the feeling we associate with being rich. That might be a sense of comfort, a sense of security and the feeling of excitement at being able to travel and do what you want. When you ask, make sure you are asking for the right things.

2. Allow

This step is often harder because it is not us doing it. This is the universe's part of the process. We need to trust the universe. The universe will organise how and when it will all happen. We will explore this idea more later on.

3. Receive

This is the exciting part. We actually achieve a goal. We

are grateful. We can continually repeat this process. We build the confidence. Success breeds success.

Meditation

It is important to relax your mind on a regular basis. People do meditation in many different ways. I just sit quietly for 10 to 15 minutes each morning. When I first started to meditate, I thought it was a little strange and worried that my mind would go off somewhere. It is not like that for me at all. I take deep breaths, try to clear my mind of thoughts and just relax.

Some mornings it works better than others. What I do find is that often ideas pop into my mind. I have learned to act quickly on these ideas. Other times if I have a question or a decision to make, I will think on it quietly during this time and usually an answer will occur to me within a couple of days.

Inner Self

We come equipped with our own compass to what Stephen Covey refers to as our True North. Our feelings let us know if we are headed in the correct direction. We are wired to be happy. If you are not happy, you are not headed in the correct direction.

Unfortunately many of us were brought up with almost the opposite teachings. If you are having fun or you are enjoying something, it must be bad. If you feel guilty when you are spending money, having fun or the like, you may have absorbed these kinds of beliefs and attitudes.

I repeat, you are wired to be happy. That is your true state. To reach your potential, you need to trust the feelings you get in your solar plexus. It always alerts you when you stray off course.

Practise feeling positive, happy feelings. Try to feel the way you will when you receive or reach what you've asked for. Act, speak and think as if you are receiving it now. This is a powerful step in using the Law of Attraction. When you feel like you already have it, the universe manifests it.

Sometimes people think they are thinking positively about what they want, but in fact what they are really thinking about is the lack of having what they want. They think, 'It hasn't happened yet; where is it?' This concentration on lack is the dominant thought.

In many circumstances it can be difficult to feel like you already have the money or whatever you have asked for. Until your thoughts and feelings are aligned with what you want, you will not receive it.

The universe works in its own time. If you start worrying about the time, you are sending a message to the universe that you lack faith.

Your Wealth

The universe has an abundance of wealth to give. In our society money is the way we are gifted with wealth. You might ask, 'If it is so easy, why doesn't everyone have wealth?' It could be that they have their wealth-making magnets set to repel instead of attract. There are a few things you can do to make sure your wealth magnet is set to its full potential.

We talked about the influence your family and friends might have on your attitude to money and wealth. Did you hear comments like 'money is evil' and negative statements about rich people?

The Bible is often misquoted as saying, 'Money is the root of all evil'. What it actually says is 'The love of money is the root of all evil'.

Being rich and having money is a good thing. You can do great things for yourself and for others. You don't need to feel guilty at all.

Regularly saying affirmations can help you build a new relationship with money and wealth.

- I am and will always be wealthy.
- I am continuously increasing my wealth with every passing day.
- It makes me feel excited to know that abundance and wealth are   available to me.
- Being wealthy fills me with total contentment and pure joy.
- Anything that I do always produces a prosperous growth in my wealth.

Chapter 5: Your Positive Mindset

Mindset

Mindset is a simple idea discovered by world-renowned Stanford University psychologist Carol Dweck in decades of research on achievement and success—a simple idea that makes all the difference. In a fixed mindset, people will believe the basic qualities, like intelligence or talent, are simply fixed traits. They spend their time documenting their intelligence or talent instead of developing them. They also believe that talent alone creates success— without effort. They're wrong.

In a growth mindset, people believe that their most basic abilities can be developed through dedication and hard work; that brains and talent are just the starting point. This view creates a love of learning and resilience that is essential for great accomplishment. Virtually all great people have had these qualities.

Sometime in your life you have known someone, perhaps yourself, who had a goal and who reached it. It doesn't really matter what we are talking about: it could have been getting a good mark on a test, going out with someone you wanted to or getting a car space outside the front of the venue.

We've all had the experience of wanting something and then getting it, no matter how big or small. What helped us get what we wanted? It's most likely it included determination, focus, confidence, passion and faith.

After all that we talked about concerning the Law of Attraction, if we used all of these qualities for one specific goal and we got what we wanted, why don't we apply them more often and get more of the things we want in life?

I suggest because the thoughts we have create a big difference between something we perceive as easily attainable and something that seems harder, like becoming a millionaire.

When we really want something, we don't allow anything to get in the way. So when we analyse it, the difference is not the process that prevents us from doing what we want. It's a mindset that says to us, 'This is going to be too hard'. Actually it's only as difficult as we make it out to be.

It's Easy

Perhaps the hardest part of learning how to be a millionaire is unlearning the belief that it is difficult. In fact it's as easy as anything else you have really wanted to learn about and have had success with.

Whatever goal you're trying to reach, focus on believing it won't be as difficult as you might have previously thought. It's a good idea to practise with a few things that might be just a small stretch of your current beliefs. See how you go. It will be a test of whether you have managed to overcome any negative thoughts around money you may have had.

For example if you have struggled to pay utility bills in the past, then in your quiet reflective times remind yourself either by thinking or saying out loud, 'I am continually improving in how I manage my accounts. I am able to pay my utility bills on time'.

If a little voice inside your head says, 'No, you don't'. You need to take a deep breath and rephrase and repeat until that little voice becomes fainter and fainter. If you include words like 'improving' or 'becoming more skilled', that voice has less to argue with than if you just think 'I will pay …'

Lots of people believe that good things are scarce. They act as if there was a limit to abundance. It is simply not true. Look around you, there is abundance everywhere. Celebrate your success as well as the successes of those around you. Don't for one moment think that because others are making money, that it will in some way limit the money available to you.

Scarcity thinking will result in scarcity. Thinking of abundance will result in abundance. The scarcity model, constantly looking around for the problems, overlooks and discounts what's right in front of us. We have to constantly remind ourselves to look for 'what's right' in our lives instead of 'what's wrong'.

Get rid of any tendency you have to be the 'Woe is me' or 'The sky is falling' type of person. The glass is always half full.

Lots of people focus on problems, on the negative, on what's not working. The simple truth is that what we focus on expands. If you focus on what's going wrong in your life, you will get more of what's wrong in your life. If you focus more on what's going right in your life, you'll get more of what's right.

High Vibrations

Everything in the universe moves and vibrates. Everything is vibrating at one speed or another. Nothing rests. Everything you see around you is vibrating at one frequency or another—and so are you.

Your frequency is different from other things in the universe. That's why it seems you are separated from what you see around you—people, animals, plants and so on. The truth is you are not separated; you are in fact living in an ocean of energy. We are all connected at the lowest level, which is called the unified field.

Everything has its own vibrational frequency—the table, the car, the desk, even our thoughts and feelings. A table may look solid and still, but within the table there are millions of millions of subatomic particles running around and popping with energy. The table is pure energy and movement. We cannot see this, so it appears separate and solid to us. It is actually an illusion.

Formula

Oprah tells how she got a part in the movie *The Colour Purple*. It was all about how she was thinking, feeling and drawing it into her life by putting all her emotions behind it. She used the formula, thought + emotions = attraction, to develop a positive mindset to get what she wanted. She succeeded and was in the film.

Low Energy

I'm sure you have experienced the feeling of being with a person who has low energy. You may have been feeling terrific, but after being with them for a while, you felt as though some of your energy had been sucked out of you.

Being around negative people has this effect. It is much better to be with positive, high-energy people as much as you can. That is why it is important to choose your friends well. If any of your family members have this effect on your energy level, limit the time you spend with them.

If you want to attract something, you need to be at the same vibrational frequency as what you want. Things on the same vibrational frequency make themselves known to each other. They vibrate on the same frequency. When we send out signals on a certain frequency through our thoughts and emotions, the universe responds to us with anything and everything that resonates with that frequency.

That is why it is important to vibrate with the feelings of already having received what you want instead of vibrating with what we are doubtful of, fearful of and so on.

Money as Energy

Think about money as energy. When you pay out or receive money, it's really a measure of the value of the energy you are exchanging. If you're getting $30 an hour, you're saying that the energy you're putting out to create the value that you're creating is worth $30 an hour. If you want to make more, figure out how to raise the energy that you are putting out and how to deliver more value to others at the same time.

Wealth Mindset

You have to believe that you deserve wealth. If you don't believe that, you will overlook countless opportunities. If you don't believe you deserve wealth, you will sabotage your own efforts. If you're wanting to attract wealth but don't believe you deserve it, it's like driving a car and pressing both the accelerator and the brake at the same time. It just doesn't work.

Develop an opportunity consciousness. Look around and start the habit of asking yourself, 'How can I add more value? How can I make things faster, easier, quicker, less hassle and more fun for people? How can I make money solving this challenge? What can I do to solve this problem and make money doing it?' The bigger the problem is to solve, the more wealth will pour into your life. The more you serve others, the more wealth you will achieve.

Think of others. The more you make your time and life valuable to others, the more wealth you will have. Organise your life to matter more. Develop more valuable skills, spend more time with high achievers and focus on serving people.

To keep your mind healthy, you need to make sure you only put good things into it. If you put garbage in, you will get garbage results. Monitor your own internal dialogue and monitor what other people are saying to you, especially regarding money matters, finances and wealth.

Control

There are many stories, especially during bad times like war, when people used their mind control to help them survive. Others can do terrible things to your body and possessions, but you are in control of your mind. You have a choice when obstacles or bad things occur. You can strengthen your resolve to get through things. Imagine you are out of your body, looking down on yourself going through whatever trial you are facing. Tell yourself down there that you can survive this; that you won't let anything or anybody destroy your dream.

Sharpen the Saw

One of Stephen Covey's habits is 'Sharpen the Saw'. This is a metaphor, meaning our minds are the saw and we have to work to keep them sharp. If you have ever tried to saw through wood with a blunt saw, you would understand why regularly sharpening it is essential.

The same goes for your mind. Leaning does not come to a stop when you finish school or college. You need to keep sharpening your mind forever. He suggests the wisdom literature, meaning it should be good stuff. It should motivate you to be the best person, friend and citizen that you can be.

I have only touched the surface of many of these topics in this book. To have the best You Inc. possible, you need to keep learning. If reading is not your thing, now there are thousands of audiobooks, TED talks and podcasts.
I always listen to books when I walk. Instead of music in the car, you can play motivational speakers.

Chapter 6: Understand Your Numbers

Why Numbers Are Important

Achieving many of your goals, if not all of them, is going to be dependent on numbers—your numbers. There are numbers for health, and there are number for wealth. If you think about it, there are numbers of consequence in every aspect of your life.

If you are serious about making money and being healthy enough to live to enjoy it, there will be some vital ones for you to know.

To be financially healthy, you need to learn all the numbers connected with building wealth. If mathematics was not a favourite subject at school, you may to tend to steer away from number talk and glaze over when people around you discuss them. That has to change.

Terms and numbers for income and expenses will be top of your 'What's Hot List'. You will learn to recognise the different types of interest; the relevance of interest rates for borrowing and saving; numbers associated with assets and liabilities and whether or not you have any of them.

Many of these numbers you are going to learn are interrelated, and that is why it is crucial to understand the way all the numbers fit together.

Be a Smart Cookie

Smart cookies know their numbers. They know what their real costs and earnings are. They make their money work for them. You can be a smart cookie too.

Remember how we said that success leaves clues. Look at the successful people you know and consider about how well they know the important numbers in their businesses and lives. Sometimes we hear of celebrities who employ someone to know the numbers for them. Unfortunately that doesn't always go well as the employees can steal from them because the celebrities don't keep watch on and know their own numbers.

It is not difficult. Make a promise to yourself that you will always know your own numbers. Do not rely on anyone else to do if for you. It is fine to have a financial adviser, but you need to insist that they explain it all, so you can understand your own money situation. The same applies to a bookkeeper. They can do the manual work but under your direction.

More Than Money

Financial health and getting rich are probably all you want to concentrate on at the moment, but I want to warn you that you also need to be mindful of the numbers you should know to maintain your physical health.

When you are striving hard to reach a goal, it is easy to forget all the other things in your life. That is why I encouraged you to have goals in the seven areas. I didn't do this in my early years, and I worked much too hard, and my health suffered. It is pointless being rich and not being able to enjoy it. Keep your wheel balanced.

During your next visit to the doctor, ask about the numbers you should know. There are optimum numbers for steps per day, sugar levels, blood pressure and eyesight, for example. Do you know which shots you have had and how long they last?

We talked about your being your own company. As boss of that company, you need to take pride in knowing everything about You Inc., so if someone randomly asks you any number question, you instantly have the answer.

The mantra to remember is 'Know Your Numbers'.

Let's Talk Numbers

To be able to discuss your numbers, we need to build your financial literacy, so you will be confident and comfortable when speaking with professionals about your finances. This may mean learning some new terms and skills. These money management skills have the potential to improve your financial and personal outcomes substantially.

Today's financial world is complex. Financial literacy helps us navigate a course through this complexity to make effective decisions about earning, spending, borrowing and saving.

Assets and Liabilities

You need financial literacy to be and stay safe. I learned this lesson much later in life by reading Robert T. Kiyosaki's book *Rich Dad Poor Dad*. He stresses how it is essential to know the difference between assets and liabilities. In simple terms he explains assets are what earn you money and liabilities are what cost you money.

To build wealth you need to increase the number of assets you have. Kiyosaki tries to motivate his readers to purchase assets while keeping the liabilities (expenses) to a bare minimum. He says that poor people remain poor because they do the opposite. They pile up their liabilities and have zero assets so that their balance sheets and income statements look out of kilter.

An easy rule of thumb is that assets go up in value and liabilities go down. If you buy something, it can appreciate in value, which means its value goes up. Some artwork for example may go up in value, so the amount on your asset side of the balance sheet does increase, but you receive no income from the artwork. You have to sell it to realise or benefit from the increase in value. Other things you buy may depreciate, which means that they go down in value. Most personal items come under this heading.

We often use the word 'investment' when we buy a particularly classic or expense piece of clothing, although it is unlikely we will sell it at a later date and receive more than we paid for it. In this circumstance what we really mean is that it may save us money because it will last a while and not go out of fashion.

So it is very unlikely we can count any of this type of item as an asset. Although having said that, I have read of a girl who started renting out her 'It' handbag. That might be considered a business, not an asset, because I doubt that the handbag would increase in value, as it would be so worn.

Passive Income

Passive income is money we receive from having the asset. This is different to the money we make by selling the asset. This is money we receive on a regular basis as if we were being paid in a job. Having lots of passive income is what we will be aiming for when we discuss budgets later. Passive income generally comes from having investments.

A simple form of passive income can be the interest the bank pays you when you lend them your cash. That is actually what you are doing when you deposit your money in some kind of savings account with the bank. The income they pay you is called interest. The rates of interest the bank is prepared to pay you vary. It depends on factors such as how much you are prepared to deposit and for how long you agree to leave it there without touching it. If it is only a few hundred dollars or less and you withdraw some and then deposit some on a regular basis, you will receive the lowest interest rate.

In a later chapter we will discuss how you can borrow to start accumulating assets, which produce passive income.

Interest Rates

One of the ways the bank makes its money is by using the money that all the depositors have put into the bank to lend to others at a higher interest rate. As a simple example, if you deposited one thousand dollars and the bank interest rate for deposits was 2.4% p.a., you would earn $24 dollars in passive income at the end of the year.

In real life it would be a little better than the example as the bank usually pays the interest they owe you each month, which means that in the second month your deposit would have grown to $1,002, so at the end of that month you would receive interest on the new amount. This is called compound interest.

The bank lends your $1,000 to a borrower and charges them 6.4% interest. The difference is the income for the bank. The borrower agrees to pay the bank back over an agreed period, and each time a payment is made, the interest due will decrease as the amount still outstanding decreases. The banks may calculate interest on a daily basis but pay it monthly or at the end of an agreed fixed term.

Different banks offer different interest rates for different purposes. If you are borrowing for a car, the term of the loan would be different than if you are borrowing to buy property.

Credit Cards

Another way banks and other financial institutions lend you money is by allowing you to use one of their credit cards. In fact they encourage you to use their credit cards. The interest rates they charge on credit cards can be significantly higher than they charge if you take out a direct loan from the bank.

The Value of Money

Your cash changes value over time. If you had a $100 note in a box at home, even though there would still be $100 in the box in ten years time, the value would be much less. At the beginning of the ten-year period the groceries that $100 could buy would be far more than ten years later.

That change in value is called inflation. To build wealth, your money needs to grow at a rate, which is more than inflation. If inflation is 3% each year and you are earning 2%, the value of your money is going down even though you are receiving interest and your total is going up. You will hear people say that their salaries are not keeping up with inflation. They may be earning more dollars each year, but because prices go up at a faster rate, they can buy less with their money.

So we need to increase the total value of our money to grow wealth, not just have a bigger number.

Crunch Time

By looking at your current situation, we will be able to ascertain how your target wealth can be reached. We will be able to look at some strategies to help make it happen. You need to know and understand basic financial facts about yourself.

To be in charge of your own destiny you need to be able to recite the totals of all income and expenses—this is what this exercise is all about. Until you face the absolute truth about your situation, you cannot move forward in a positive way.

Current Income

'What do you earn?' seems a simple question, but often it is not so easy to answer off the top of your head. If you are working for someone else, convert your wages or salary into an amount per year, for example $50,000 p.a. (short for *per annum*, meaning per year). You need to know if this amount includes all additional benefits you may receive.

If you have begun working for yourself, the answer may be a little more complex as you might have decided not to take much money out of the business in the beginning. You will need to do a business plan for the business which projects the money you should be able to take each year as the business grows.

For new entrepreneurs these become a second lot of numbers they have to know and understand. Small businesses often fail in the first few years because the owners do not watch and understand their numbers. The numbers always tell the story as it is.

Credit History

What kind of credit history do you have? It is important to build a good credit history. Those unpaid power or telephone bills from years back can stop you getting a loan or a mortgage. This can be a shock three years later. Who knew they mattered so much? Young people need to be taught how credit checks work in their early teens so that they understand the consequences of their actions later on.

Credit cards. Do you have any? What are the limits on them? What interest rates are you paying? Even if the amount owing is zero dollars, the lender counts the limit on the card as debt. This is because you are able to run up that amount of debt at any time. It may be advisable to lower the limits on your credit cards.

Other loans—do you have a car loan or any other type of loan?

Saving History

Savings? Do you have any? Do you regularly save? Could you stretch yourself a little and regularly save more? Lenders like to see a history of savings.

It would have been great if when you got your first part-time job, you opened a savings account just for saving the deposit for your first investment property. That probably did not happen back then, as it was not usual to give girls that advice. It should have been then, and it should be now. If you do not have such an account, you should start one as soon as possible. Regular saving is essential for your success.

Living Expenses

Rent—how much per month? Even if you live at your parents' home for free, a lender will calculate a rental amount as an expense for you. If you have been living for free, have you been saving the amount you would have had to pay for rent elsewhere? It is a lost opportunity otherwise.

General spending—how do you spend your money? I think it is a worthwhile exercise to really understand how you usually spend your money. By keeping a record over a couple of months, you will be able to see the percentage you spend on entertainment, travel, cosmetics and clothes, for example.

Know Your Finances

Each of us is different, and we each will have different priorities for our money. The aim here is for you to know your own finances and how you generally use your money. It may shock you how much you actually spend in some categories. Having this knowledge is invaluable in helping you set priorities. It will also show you very clearly where you can find some savings. Remember—know your numbers.

Your Current Income

I wasn't good at knowing exactly what I earned when I started work. It was not considered 'ladylike' to discuss salaries with colleagues. Women tended to be poor at asking for things for themselves. There was this inferred unspoken message that we should be thankful that we were being paid anything. Interestingly women would fight for those they cared about but found it uncomfortable talking about their own circumstances.

I still meet many young women who can't give an answer if asked what they earn. They may know how much they clear each pay period after tax and other things are deducted, but they don't know annual gross amount.

If you are just starting out in your own business, it can be very exciting to bank a lot of money that the business has taken, but if you don't know exactly what your outgoings or expenses are, you may actually be making a loss.

The Truth About Expenses

What do you really spend? If you're going to create wealth, it's best to understand where money goes, so that you can control it. And that takes a budget. Think of creating a budget as a financial strategy for your dreams. Doesn't that sound more appealing and more manageable?

You have to be honest with yourself here. You need to know your net pay—the amount you actually receive after tax. Hopefully it will be the money you can pay yourself from your own business or it may be the money someone else pays you. You may be already earning some passive income, so add that on the income side.

It can be a little tricky doing this exercise as some expenses are almost daily and some are perhaps only once a year. I suggest you calculate each expense per pay period. If you are paid weekly, divide any annual payments by 52, if you are paid fortnightly by 26 and if you are paid once a month, then divide by 12.

Do not make the mistake of just multiplying a weekly expense by 4 to create a monthly amount. There are more than 4 weeks in a month. To accurately convert a weekly expense into a calendar month expense (if you are paid monthly, there are 12 pays a year), you need to divide the weekly amount by 7, then multiply it by 365 to calculate how much for the whole year and then divide by 12. Monthly rent is calculated this way.

Some of your amounts will be a little shocking I am sure. I found lots of surprises when I first did mine. One shock was coffee. I used to buy two coffees a day at work plus the same on the weekend. That was at least $49 a week or sometimes a little more depending on where I was or if I had a third. That made it a $213+ monthly expense. I decided that buying a capsule coffee machine would quickly pay for itself and could help me save at least half that coffee amount.

Setting a budget is not an exercise in being mean to yourself. On the contrary, it is an exercise in helping you understand where you spend your money now so that you can be sure you are spending where it benefits you most. Use the following categories to help you understand and calculate your expenses.

Rent and Utilities

- Rent
- Heating costs
- Telephone
- Electricity/gas
- Internet/cable
- Water/sewage

Transportation

- Car repayment
- Car insurance
- Petrol
- Maintenance
- Registration
- Parking
- Public transport
- Tolls
- Other

Health

- Health insurance
- Doctor/hospital visits
- Dentist visits
- Eye care
- Prescriptions
- Over-the-counter medications

- Health clubs

Food, Clothing and Cleaning
- Essential groceries
- Non-essential groceries
- Personal care—shampoo/toothpaste/haircuts
- Home living supplies
- Work lunches
- Dining out
- Clothing
- Work clothes
- Dry cleaning

Entertainment, Education and Miscellaneous
- Education expenses
- Postage
- Leisure
- Movies out
- Other outside entertainment
- Cigarettes and alcohol
- Lottery tickets
- Other gambling
- Books, magazines and newspapers
- Weekend/day trips
- Vacation/travel
- Sports

- Birthdays/anniversaries
- Charities/church

The Balance Sheet

Calculate a total for expenses and a total for income. If your expenses exceed your income, you have just discovered you are living beyond your means, so you have two choices. Firstly you can cut back on your expenses.

A small example of cutting expenses is taking your lunch to work instead of buying it each day. We had a challenge at work to see how much could be saved in a month by doing this. The average saved in our office was just over $200 per month. The positive side effect was that a couple of people couldn't go back to the greasy take-aways they were accustomed to eating each day before the challenge.

Alternatively you can increase your income. This option is a little more difficult as you do not have any excess after paying your liabilities to help you acquire assets, which in turn would bring in additional income.

The only thing you could use is your labour. You would need to increase the amount of work you do to help increase your income.

The best result of course is to have more income than expenses. This excess can then be used to acquire assets and begin to build passive income. In the next chapter we will look at how you will begin doing this.

Chapter 7: Let Investments Do The Work

Building Your Assets

For our purposes I am only going to call things that bring you a passive income 'assets'. Technically anything of value can go in your asset column, but that doesn't help make you rich because you have to sell them to benefit from the money.

Many elderly people are asset poor. All their money is in things such as art, jewellery and antique furniture, and they may live in a mansion. However, none of these things brings in an income.

In the last chapter you calculated the excess cash you have each month, which you can use to acquire assets that bring in passive income. We are going to call these assets your 'investments'. You need to start investing now. I can hear you asking yourself how you can acquire an investment with a reasonably small amount of money.

Investing

Once we start discussing investments, you are going to discover there are lots of people out there offering you wonderful investment opportunities. I am going to take you through one type of investment, so you understand the way it works and you can then apply that knowledge to other circumstances. I want you to be able to differentiate between solid investments and more risky, speculative investments.

Begin to think in terms of passive income. You should be developing some kind of passive income as soon as possible. Passive income is something you do once and get paid multiple times for it. It is the real secret of the rich.

If you are always selling your time in exchange for money, your income is limited because your time is limited. This is important, think on it.

Be a Critical Thinker

It astounds me that so many people believe everything they are told or everything they read. You need to develop the part of your brain that says, 'Hold on a minute, does that make sense?' Your brain will often send you a signal, a 'feeling' that what you are hearing is wrong or not in your best interest. Learn to think for yourself and not always accept what others tell you as the truth.

The reason that we often get stuck with bad politicians is that people have not assessed their promises critically. Don't take things on face value, learn to think a little more. Just because a public figure or a celebrity says something doesn't make it the truth.

Sometimes it might be someone making promises about making you lots of money. It might be his latest get-rich scheme. Think about it critically, if what you are being told sound true. Does it make sense? If it is so good, why don't more people know about it?

Don't be gullible—always do some critical thinking first. If it seems to be too good to be true, that is a signal. It probably is.

I hear about women who have sent money to men they met on the internet. They want the relationship they have established to be authentic, so they turn off that part of the brain that would have prompted them to ask the hard questions.

Look around you and identify people who show that they didn't apply critical things skills. Once you become aware of the lack of it in others, it is easier to see when you might make the same mistake.

Good Debt Bad Debt

I have a Scottish background from my mother's side, and my grandmother really preached the virtues of having a no-debt status. I think it was an accepted Scottish practice that all debts were paid before the year came to a close.

There are different kinds of debt. I have come to understand that it is foolish to borrow for something that goes down in value, that is a liability. If you would like a holiday but don't have the cash to pay for it, you should not borrow the money. Using the credit card is borrowing. If it doesn't have the potential to bring in passive income, then it shouldn't happen until you can pay for it in advance. If you borrow for a liability, that's bad debt.

It does make financial sense to borrow to buy something that goes up in value. That is the premise in borrowing to buy an investment property. That's good debt. The amount you borrow is fixed, but the value of the item keeps going up.

The Investing Habit

The habit of investing is much more important than the

amount you invest. You may have to start small at first. That doesn't matter. It is the habit that counts. Regularly put money into an interest-bearing savings account, which you call your investment account. Don't be discouraged if it seems such a small amount to begin with. By starting, you are telling the universe that you are intent on investing and earning passive income by doing it.

You are saving for a deposit on an income-producing property. You only need enough for a deposit, and then you can take a mortgage to pay for the balance. You will then be using leverage to increase the amount of passive income you will be able to produce in the future.

Using Leverage

Leverage is when you use someone else's money to make money for you.

Let us look at a very simple example to demonstrate the point.

Scenario One:

You have $50,000 in a savings account. You invest it in a term deposit at the bank. You will receive interest on that deposit each year. For the sake of the example, say it is around 4% p.a. You will declare this as income and pay income tax accordingly each year. At the end of ten years, you will have about $90,000 less the amount of income tax you will have paid each year depending on your tax rate.

Scenario Two:

You use your $50,000 as a deposit on an investment property valued at $500,000. You take a mortgage for $450,000. In ten years if the property doubled in value, you would have a $1,000,000 property with a $450,000 mortgage. You would have accumulated $550,000 of equity in the property and paid no tax.

I have done this comparison to show that by having this 'good debt', you have been able to significantly increase your wealth by the leverage of someone else's (usually the bank's) money.

Of course, this example is very simplistic, as I have not calculated the buying and holding costs less rent and taxation benefits. I simply want to make the point that not all debt is bad. It is perfectly acceptable to have debt when using it to build an investment portfolio.

Investment Property

As my expertise is in residential property, I will be showing you how you will use your financial numbers to buy property and build up your capacity to generate wealth.

We will be discussing investing in residential property. You will probably be looking to borrow for a mortgage. The people or organisations lending money for mortgages are called mortgagees. Mortgagees have different criteria for self-employed and part-time workers versus full-time employees.

You will always have to have evidence of your income. Your accountant will provide your business numbers if you are running your own enterprise.

Establish a system of keeping all your records. You need to carefully separate your business expenses from your personal. If you start early with some kind or way of organising your important 'number' documents, you won't end up with that terrible example we sometimes see in TV shows when the characters has a bundle of screwed up, old, dirty receipts stuffed in a shoe box. He then expects his accountant to make sense of what has been happening.

When you buy an investment property to build wealth, there is a significant difference than when you buy a property as your home. This investment property will be an asset. Kiyosaki says that the family home is a liability as it doesn't bring you income and you have to spend money on it each year.

Technically he is wrong as your home does have value and that value will increase over time. This increase in value is called capital gains. This value is not much good to you unless you can unlock the money in it in some way. It is possible to gain access to the equity you have in the home and use it to acquire income-producing investments.

When you buy an investment property, it definitely goes in the asset column. The property will provide income for you in a variety of ways.

Technological Help

If you are a technology user, there are lots of apps to help with financial matters. There are improvements happening almost every day, so check them out. Look at mint.com and checkout OneReceipt. A service called Slice can scan all your email receipts and create a dashboard for you. Another service to help you keep expenses under control is BillGuard. If you are an Evernote user, then also look at FileThis.com. These provide a good start. Find what works best for you.

Rental Returns

This means the money you receive by renting out the property. The mortgagee will count a proportion of the rent as income when calculating if you have enough income to repay the mortgage. Rental returns are usually given as an annual percentage.

Calculating Rental Returns

The purchase price for the investment property is $500,000.
The current rent for the property is $1,720 per calendar month.

Calculate this as an annual figure, that is $1,720 x 12 = $20,640.

To calculate annual rental, return divide 20,640 by 500,000 and multiply by 100 to calculate a percentage.

In this example the rental return is 4.13%

Remember this is only part of the income you derive from the investment property.

Taxation Benefits

In some countries the governments allow you to claim some of the expenses of owning a property when assessing your taxation level. Your accountant will be able to outline if that option is available to you. Do not ever buy an investment property just because of the taxation benefits as some have done in the past. Taxation laws can be changed by governments at any time. If there is a taxation benefit, it is a bonus.

Capital Growth

The conservative view in the real estate industry is that property increases in value over time. This is called capital gain/growth. There are of course no guarantees as we saw through the Global Financial Crisis, but the conservative view is that residential property generally doubles in value in about ten+ years.

As an example of a good outcome with capital growth, look at a property purchased for $500,000 in 2015 that could be worth $1,000,000 in 2025. That means there would be $500,000 in capital gains over that time which averages out at $50,000 per year.

Sounds good, doesn't it? But remember this is a long-term exercise. You would not have that $50,000 capital gain in cash to spend each year, as you would have with the rental return and any taxation benefit. It is helpful though to understand the figure as you can then see how your asset value would be building.

Equity

To calculate the equity you have in a property, you subtract the amount of the mortgage from the current value of the property. The balance is your equity.

When you first purchase the property, the deposit you paid is your equity in the property.

If your $500,000 investment property increases in value by 10% to $550,000 after the first year, your mortgage stays the same at $450,000, but the difference is now $100,000. You have $100,000 equity in the property.

Capital gains are wonderful for the long-term investor. The increase in value is not taxed until you actually sell the property. Many investors choose not to sell but to refinance the property and take out of the property most of the increase in equity. I have observed that the investors who have created significant wealth through investment properties rarely sell. They use the increase in equity to purchase their next property and so on. By doing this, they avoid any selling costs and capital gains taxation implications.

Time Is Your Friend

The term 'investment' infers time is involved, and property investment is no different. It usually involves years, not months or days. If you need to make money from property in less than five years, then you'll be buying as a property speculator, not an investor, and this advice is not for property speculators. However, if the wealth you seek is for building financial independence for yourself in the long-term, then this applies.

Buying the First Property

- You have a regular income
- You have a good credit record
- You have saved a deposit

How much is the mortgagee likely to be willing to lend you? Mortgagees take into account your total income and outgoings to determine this figure. When you know your numbers, search for a mortgage calculator online and roughly calculate how much you can borrow.

Your Strategy

The idea is to buy the first property in a well-researched, good rental area, which has a history of solid capital growth. They do exist. Not everyone lost money during the Global Financial Crisis. Lots of people made money in real estate.

Only take advice from the appropriate professional. Everyone has an opinion about real estate, and your family will be no exception. Do your own research on the market where you are thinking of buying. With access to the internet these days you can find out lots of information, such as history, current rental prices and sale prices. Be cautious but don't be paralysed.

You may have to contribute to the mortgage payment at first, as the rent may not completely cover the repayment. The repayment will vary depending on the length of the loan your financial adviser recommends and the percentage deposit you were able to pay.

Remember rents go up but the loan amount stays the same. Within a couple of years you will be pleased to see the rental return completely covering the repayment. You can simply replicate the process if you can save enough for the next deposit or if the value of the investment property has risen, you may be able to refinance and use the increase in equity as the deposit on the next property.

It is usual with this strategy to take interest only loans. Once your portfolio starts to grow, there is a snowball effect. As a very long-term goal, you can sell one or more of the properties and pay that off the others. You will be able to own them outright at some stage. That depends on the rate of capital growth. Long before that there will be some positive cash flow from the rentals.

The clever thing is to hold on to the properties. Never sell. You avoid buying and selling costs. You can take money out of the properties by refinancing.

Many of these factors will be different in different parts of the country. This example I have shown you gives you a start with your investment thinking.

Now you need to start asking questions about where you want to buy. Don't be pushed into anything. I call this a 'sharp pencil exercise'. It is about making money. You are not buying a property you want to live in. It has to satisfy the capital growth and good rental returns criteria. It does not have to be a pretty cottage with a picket fence. That's emotional buying, which has nothing to do with investing.

Once you start making more money from your business, you might want to expand your investment portfolio. Take professional advice on the best way to structure your debt. Should it be a business debt or a personal debt? I have never liked putting the business in any kind of jeopardy. That is the question you will have to ask.

Other Investments

Stockbrokers will have a story to tell about how money can be made on the stock market. I make no comment, as I am not qualified to do so. What I will say is that the banks are fairly savvy on risk factor. The banks will usually lend a larger percentage of the total value with property as the security than they will against blue chip shares.

That difference is important because part of the secret to successfully building wealth through property investment is that you are able to use someone else's money. You make capital gains on the total value of the property, which includes the bank's share.

Freedom

You are a well-informed, independent young woman who knows that a knight on a white horse is not a financial plan. You want to be financially independent which gives you freedom.

Freedom is a mindset. It's your thoughts and actions. Don't wait to be free. Save, invest and be creative on your path to financial freedom now.

Remember—the universe is on your side. Be confident and courageous. Take pride in your achievements. It is great that as a young woman, you are showing ambition and the intelligence and drive to plan for your future. Well done and good luck with all your endeavours.

What Next?

I would like to hear of your successes and challenges. I can be contacted via my website www.toniplaninsek.com.au. I will personally answer any correspondence.

This year I will be launching a series of podcasts, which may be of interest. If you would like to be notified when they are available, there is a form on the website.

You can also register for our newsletter, which has real estate tips and articles for potential and current investors.

About the Author

Toni Planinsek is an experienced, well-qualified educator. She started her teaching career in Australia and then spent over a decade teaching in Canada, the Dominican Republic and Papua New Guinea before returning to Australia.

After several years as the principal of a leading private girls' school in Melbourne, Toni decided on a career switch. She started her own business in real estate, which she has successfully built into a large, thriving business. This change meant Toni had to learn new skills and completely change the way she planned for her future. She had to make the transition from employee to self-employed. This transition made her aware of how little women are taught about becoming financially independent as they are growing up. Generally girls are not taught the importance of building passive income.

Toni is the mother of four and the grandmother of nine. In her spare time when she is not travelling to visit family in exotic places, she enjoys reading, collecting cookbooks and learning to speak French.

Review Request

Reviews are very important to authors so if you would like to give Toni some feedback please take the time to leave a review on Amazon by scrolling down to reviews under her book.

Here is the link again:

http://www.amazon.com/Girls-Guide-Wisdom-Wealth-Financial-ebook/dp/B00XFZTSWS/ref=sr_1_1?ie=UTF8&qid=1431249057&sr=8-1&keywords=a+girls%27+guide+to+wisdom+and+wealth

This is Toni's second book, and she is planning more to come. You can learn more about Toni at www.toniplaninsek.com.au or contact her directly at toni@planinsekproperty.com.au

www.ingramcontent.com/pod-product-compliance
Lightning Source LLC
Chambersburg PA
CBHW070807180526
45168CB00002B/517